THAILAND

COUNTRY EXPLORERS

Madeline Donaldson

Lerner Publications Company • Minneapolis

To Jane Anne, still my dear friend after more than fifty years!

Lerner Publications Company
A division of Lerner Publishing Group, Inc.
241 First Avenue North
Minneapolis, MN 55401 U.S.A.

Website address: www.lernerbooks.com

Library of Congress Cataloging-in-Publication Data

Donaldson, Madeline.
    Thailand / by Madeline Donaldson.
        p.   cm. — (Country explorers)
    Includes index.
    ISBN 978–0–7613–6414–6 (lib. bdg. : alk. paper)
    1. Thailand—Juvenile literature. I. Title.
    DS563.5.D646 2012
    959.3—dc22   2011005813

Manufactured in the United States of America
1 – PP – 7/15/11

Table of Contents

Welcome!

You've reached Thailand! This country is in Southeast Asia. Myanmar sits northwest of Thailand. Laos curves along the northern and eastern borders. Cambodia lies to the east. A long strip of southern Thailand is called the Malay Peninsula. This strip of Thailand meets Malaysia in the far south. The Andaman Sea touches the western side of the strip. And the Gulf of Thailand laps against the eastern side.

This fishing village is on the Andaman Sea in southern Thailand.

4

N

MYANMAR

LAOS

THAILAND

DOI
INTHANON

Chiang
Mai

PING RIVER

WANG RIVER

YOM RIVER

NAN RIVER

MEKONG RIVER

CENTRAL
PLAIN

KHORAT
PLATEAU

CHI RIVER

Nakhon
Ratchasima

PING
RIVER

MUN RIVER

CHAO PHRAYA
RIVER

Nonthaburi

Bangkok

Muang
Boran

CAMBODIA

ANDAMAN
SEA

ISTHMUS OF KRA

GULF
OF
THAILAND

MALAY
PENINSULA

Phuket

MALAYSIA

mountains
plain
plateau
★ country's capital
● city
⁘ ancient ruins

MILES

0   100   200

0   100   200   300

KILOMETERS

Wide and Thin

The northern, eastern, and central parts of Thailand are very wide. Mountains and rain forests stand out in northern Thailand. The Central Plain lies to the south. East of this plain is the Khorat Plateau. The long, thin Malay Peninsula hangs down from the Central Plain.

Rain forests cover the mountains of northern Thailand.

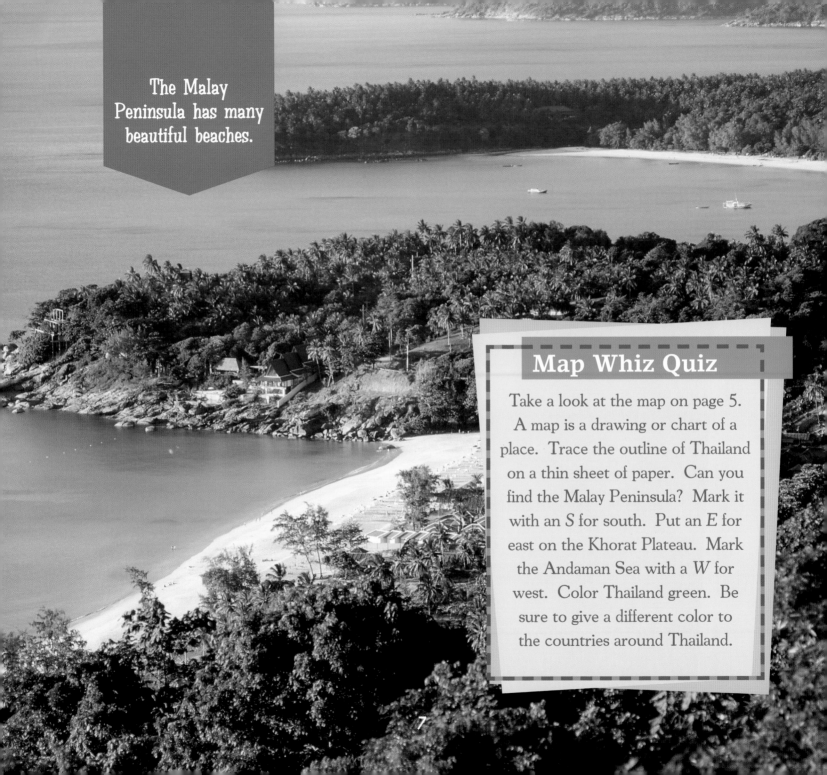

The Malay Peninsula has many beautiful beaches.

Map Whiz Quiz

Take a look at the map on page 5. A map is a drawing or chart of a place. Trace the outline of Thailand on a thin sheet of paper. Can you find the Malay Peninsula? Mark it with an *S* for south. Put an *E* for east on the Khorat Plateau. Mark the Andaman Sea with a *W* for west. Color Thailand green. Be sure to give a different color to the countries around Thailand.

Northern and Eastern Thailand

The northern mountains border Myanmar and Laos. The mountains get lower as they reach to the south. Then the mountains turn into foothills. They lead to the Central Plain. The Ping, the Wang, the Yom, and the Nan rivers flow from the mountains. They meet to form the big Chao Phraya River.

The Chao Phraya River is very important to Thailand.

8

These temples are on the top of Doi Inthanon.

Doi Inthanon

The highest point in the northern mountains is Doi Inthanon. It rises to 8,514 feet (2,595 meters).

The Khorat Plateau stands out in eastern Thailand. This area is high, flat, and dry. The land here is hard to farm. The Chi and Mun rivers flow through the plateau. Water from these rivers helps rice grow. The Mekong River forms the plateau's border with Laos.

Central Plain

The Central Plain reaches from the Gulf of Thailand to the foothills of the northern mountains. This large, flat area is perfect for growing rice, maize, and sugarcane.

The Central Plain grows so much rice, it is called the "rice bowl" of Thailand.

The Chao Phraya River flows through the plain. Canals, called *khlongs*, help carry water to the rice fields. Khlongs also give local Thai a way to get around.

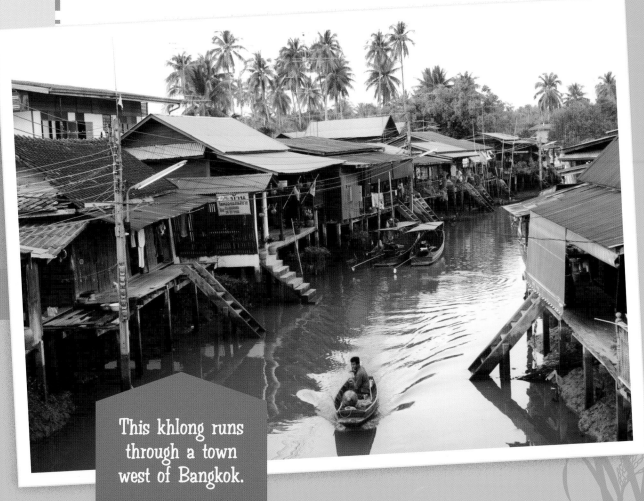

This khlong runs through a town west of Bangkok.

11

Southern Thailand

The Isthmus of Kra links the Central Plain to the Malay Peninsula. An isthmus is a narrow strip of land that connects two larger areas of land. The peninsula has lowlands along the coasts. The lowlands let farmers grow rice, fruits, coconuts, and cotton. Some farmers also raise orchids.

These workers are picking pineapples on a lowland farm.

Visitors flock to Thailand's southern islands. Phuket is one of the main islands to visit. People enjoy the beaches and warm weather.

13

A Hot, Wet Land

Temperatures in Thailand run from mild to hot. Winters are cool and dry. They begin in November and last until February. Winter temperatures range from 50 to 80°F (10 to 27°C). March through May is the hot season. Temperatures can reach higher than 100°F (38°C).

Heavy rains flooded this village in eastern Thailand.

Winds called monsoons arrive between June and October. Monsoons bring lots of rain. The mountains and the Central Plain get about 60 inches (152 centimeters). About 50 inches (127 cm) fall in the Khorat Plateau. Southern Thailand gets more than 100 inches (254 cm).

Tsunamis

Tsunamis are huge waves. Earthquakes far out at sea send the waves toward coastal areas. In 2004, these powerful waves damaged Thailand's southern coasts. Many people were killed. And the waves wiped out some coastal areas.

The 2004 tsunami flattened this Thai village on an island in the Andaman Sea.

Elephants Rule!

Thailand is home to many animals. Gibbons, water buffalo, black bears, and snakes are some of them. But Asian elephants have a special place in Thailand's history.

Gibbons like this one live in the forests of Thailand.

In the old days, warriors rode elephants into battle. Later, the animals became important for bringing logs out of the thick northern rain forests. These days, most elephants are honored as smart, gentle giants. They have special trainers and camps where they can live in safety.

National Elephant Day

This day is celebrated on March 13. People show respect and support for elephants. The elephants also get a special blessing on this day.

Elephants enjoy a buffet of fruit and vegetables on National Elephant Day.

Siam to Thailand

Thailand has been a country for hundreds of years. Its rulers have always been kings. The country often fought with its neighbors to stay free. In the late 1700s, a new king named the kingdom Siam. The people were called Siamese. These names came from outside rulers.

This painting shows a 1767 battle in central Thailand.

The word *Thai* means "free people." This is the name the people call themselves. In 1939, the Thai government changed the name of the country to Thailand.

King of Thailand

King Bhumibol (Rama IX) has been king since 1946! He is the world's longest-serving king. He has set up local projects that have helped the Thai in many ways. The Thai respect him and his family a great deal.

A group of Thai women pray for King Bhumibol.

Thailand's People

Most of Thailand's people are Thai. People from China, Laos, and Cambodia have also settled in Thailand. A small number of Malays live in the south.

Thai are known to be very welcoming. They smile often and want to be helpful. They have strong respect for older people. They try to stay happy and avoid anger.

Thai Don'ts

Thai can put up with a lot. But here are some things to avoid if you visit.

· Don't make fun of the king and the royal family.
· Don't touch someone's head. It is considered the holiest part of the body.
· Don't point your feet at someone or something. The feet are the least holy part of the body.

The Thai Language

Thai is the country's official language. The language is more than its words and letters. The way a person says a word is important.

This menu is written in Thai.

Thai has five ways to say a word. They are called tones. The five tones are mid, low, high, falling, and rising. The same word in a different tone can have a very different meaning. In written Thai, the tone to use is marked above the letter.

Say It in Thai!

hello	sawatdee	sah-waht-DEE
good-bye	lar korn	lah KAHRN
please	dai proht	die PROHT
thank you	khobkhun	cob-KOON
yes	chai	CHAY
no	mai chai	my CHAY

A girl prays before an image of the Buddha at a temple in eastern Thailand.

Buddhism

Most Thai are Buddhists. Siddhartha Gautama founded this religion. He is called the Buddha. Buddhists believe in a cycle of death and rebirth. The Buddha's teachings help people to lead a moral life. This leads to peace and happiness.

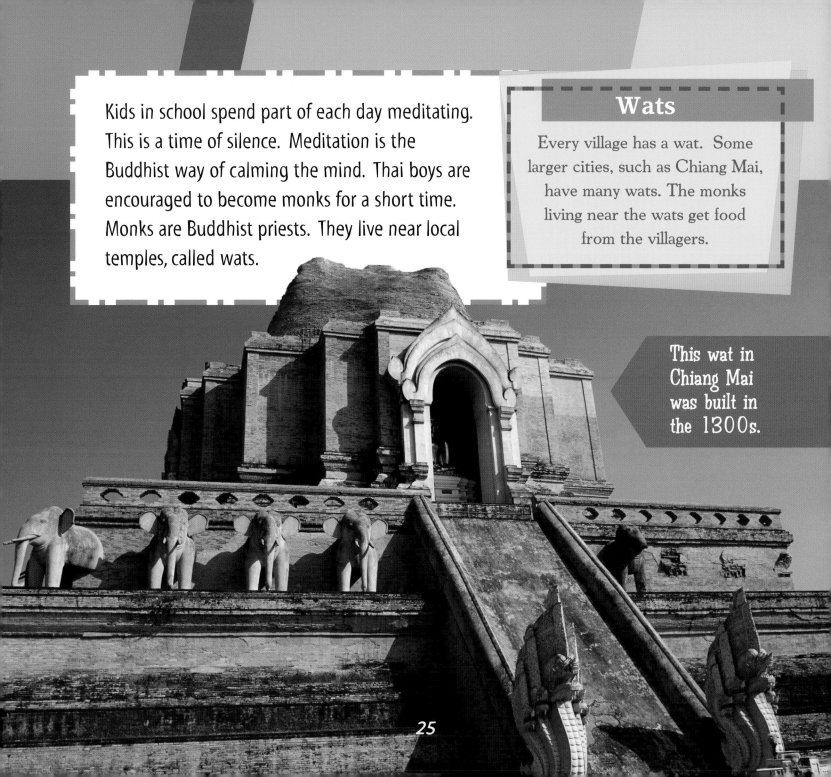

Kids in school spend part of each day meditating. This is a time of silence. Meditation is the Buddhist way of calming the mind. Thai boys are encouraged to become monks for a short time. Monks are Buddhist priests. They live near local temples, called wats.

Wats

Every village has a wat. Some larger cities, such as Chiang Mai, have many wats. The monks living near the wats get food from the villagers.

This wat in Chiang Mai was built in the 1300s.

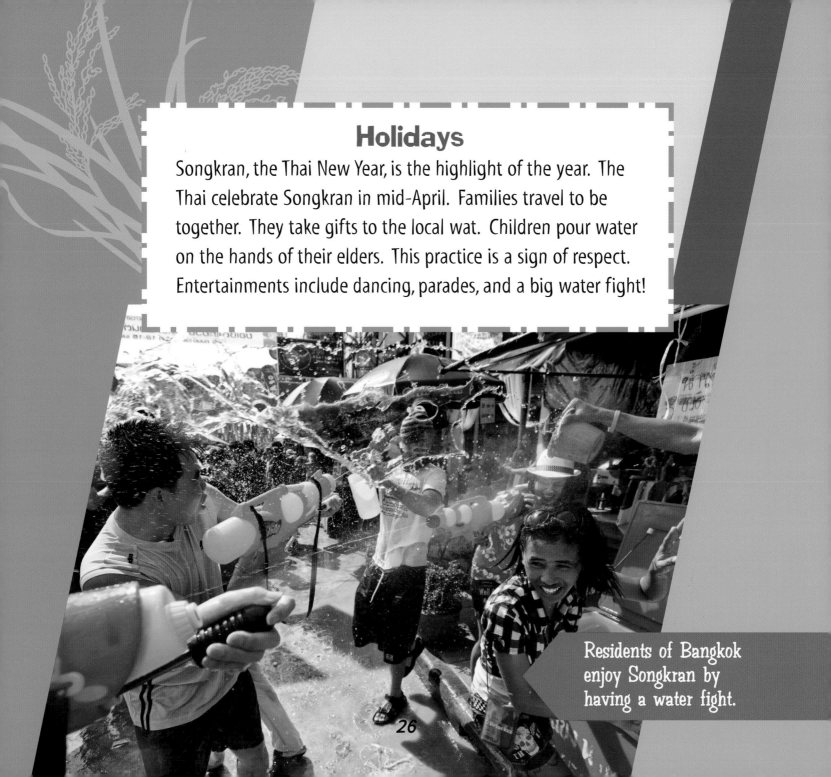

Holidays

Songkran, the Thai New Year, is the highlight of the year. The Thai celebrate Songkran in mid-April. Families travel to be together. They take gifts to the local wat. Children pour water on the hands of their elders. This practice is a sign of respect. Entertainments include dancing, parades, and a big water fight!

Residents of Bangkok enjoy Songkran by having a water fight.

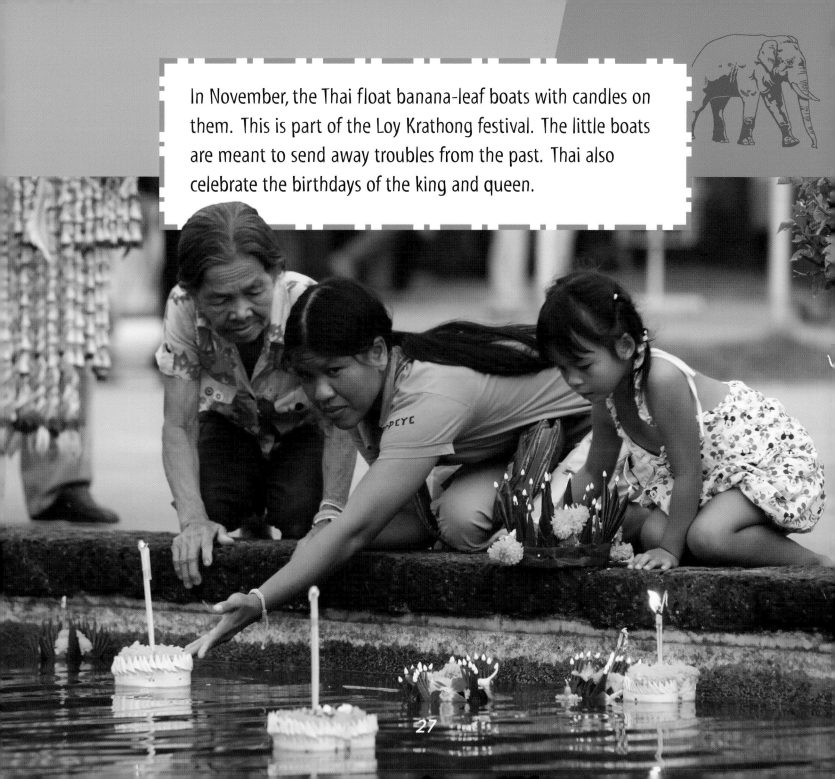

In November, the Thai float banana-leaf boats with candles on them. This is part of the Loy Krathong festival. The little boats are meant to send away troubles from the past. Thai also celebrate the birthdays of the king and queen.

Thai Cities

One of every three Thai lives in cities. The largest is the capital city of Bangkok. It lies on the Chao Phraya River. Khlongs once crisscrossed the city. People and goods traveled on them. These days, only a few khlongs remain. The others were filled in to make streets.

Nakhon Ratchasima is a city in northeastern Thailand. Chiang Mai in northern Thailand draws many visitors to its historic wats. Flowers and fruits have made Nonthaburi a market center.

Dear Aunt Mary,
We just got back from the Grand Palace. It's a huge group of buildings in Bangkok. The Thai kings used to live there. One of the buildings is the Wat Phra Kaeo. Our guide said it's a special place for Thai people. It holds a statue of the Buddha made of a green stone called jasper.
Talk to you soon!
Robert

Grand Palace

Country Life

Two out of three Thai live in the countryside. All the members of a family make their home in the same village. Sometimes the whole family lives in one house. In other villages, several homes are grouped together. Most villages have a wat and a school.

An elected leader keeps village records. That leader is called the *phu yai ban*. He or she may also settle small troubles. The leader's role is to help villagers to live together happily.

These Hmong children are wearing traditional clothes.

Getting Around

Thailand's roads and railways connect all parts of the country. People usually ride buses to go long distances. In the countryside, motorbikes or bicycles are good for short trips. People going to the same place may share a *songthaew*. This is a pickup truck with benches in the bed for seating.

A songthaew is a pickup truck that is used as a taxi.

Within cities, people get around on foot, in cars, or by light rail. Some people still use canals to travel. Visitors might take a *tuk-tuk*, a three-wheeled cart.

Tuk-tuks share the road with buses and automobiles in Bangkok.

33

Family Life

Thai kids learn respect for their elders
from an early age. They also learn how
to get along with others. Kids have
chores. They may feed the family's
livestock or take care of younger kids.

This boy is feeding
his family's pigs.

The father typically leads a Thai family. Mothers often manage the family's money. Older kids take part in family talks about important matters. Younger Thai gladly care for aging family members.

A wai greeting, shown here, is a sign of respect.

Tom yum goong
is spicy and sour.

Let's Eat!

Spices like garlic and chilies help to make Thai food very hot! *Nam pla* is an aged fish sauce. It also gives dishes a hot taste. Pad Thai (stir-fried noodles) is a favorite Thai dish. A lemony shrimp soup called *tom yum goong* is another. Fruits, such as pineapples, mangoes, papayas, and coconuts, are also popular.

Rice is served with every meal. In the Khorat Plateau, people like sticky rice. They roll the rice into balls and serve it with fried meats, including frog and lizard! In other parts of Thailand, people prefer steamed rice. Pork, beef, chicken, or vegetables may top the rice.

37

The Arts

Thai dancing is graceful. Several pairs of dancers perform in step to the music. They wear colorful traditional clothing. Sometimes the dancers carry candles or wear long nails.

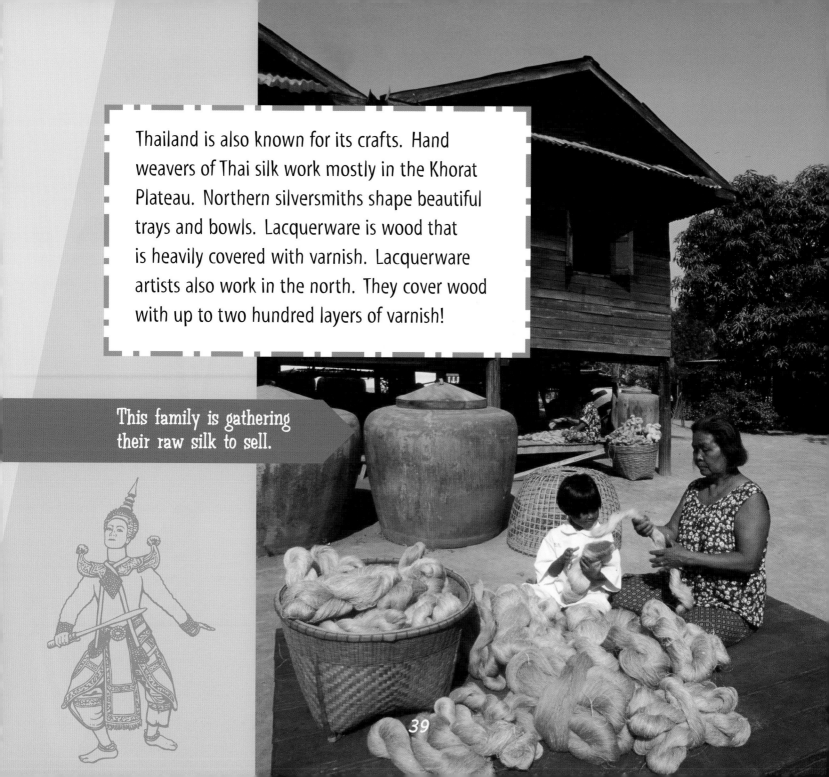

Thailand is also known for its crafts. Hand weavers of Thai silk work mostly in the Khorat Plateau. Northern silversmiths shape beautiful trays and bowls. Lacquerware is wood that is heavily covered with varnish. Lacquerware artists also work in the north. They cover wood with up to two hundred layers of varnish!

This family is gathering their raw silk to sell.

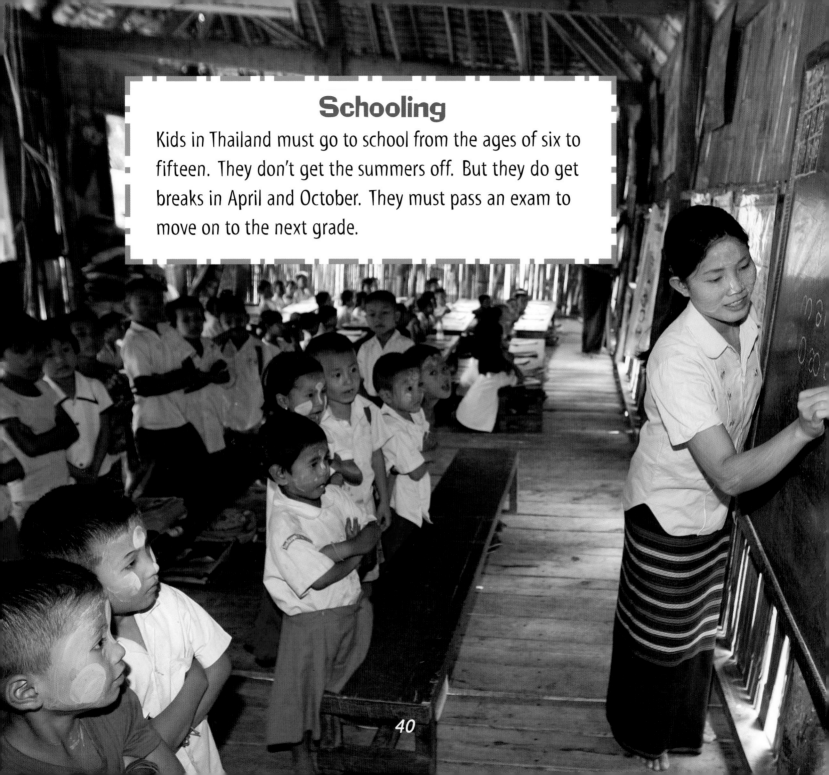

Schooling

Kids in Thailand must go to school from the ages of six to fifteen. They don't get the summers off. But they do get breaks in April and October. They must pass an exam to move on to the next grade.

Kids take classes in math, history, Buddhism, English, computers, and music. They wear uniforms. But kids don't wear shoes when inside the school building.

King Chulalongkorn (Rama V)

This ruler set up the first schools for ordinary Thai. He took many other steps to make Thailand a modern country. The people honor him for this work.

King Chulalongkorn ruled in the late 1800s and early 1900s.

Truly Thai Sports

Takraw players use their feet, heads, and legs to keep a straw ball in the air. *Muay Thai*, or Thai boxing, is a form of martial arts. Two players face each other in a ring. The boxers use their elbows, knees, and feet to defeat the opponent.

Takraw is like soccer and volleyball combined.

Twin sisters practice Muay Thai at a school outside of Bangkok.

Women Go Gold

Male Thai boxers have won four gold medals at the Olympic Games. But women have kept pace. Thai women have won gold in weightlifting. They have also become a force in Olympic tae kwon do matches.

Thai kids like to play soccer and basketball. Kite flying is also very popular. Skilled flyers try to knock their opponents' kites from the sky during contests!

THE FLAG OF THAILAND

Thailand's flag is red, white, and blue. It has five bands. The top and bottom bands are red. They stand for Thailand. The second and fourth bands are white. They stand for the Buddhist faith. The middle blue band stands for the royal family. King Rama VI made this flag official in 1917.

FAST FACTS

FULL COUNTRY NAME: Kingdom of Thailand

AREA: 198,116 square miles (513,118 square kilometers), or about the size of Arizona and Utah combined

MAIN LANDFORMS: northern mountains, Central Plain, Khorat Plateau, Malay Peninsula, Isthmus of Kra

MAJOR RIVERS: Chao Phraya, Chi, Mekong, Mun, Nan, Ping, Wang, Yom

ANIMALS AND THEIR HABITATS: black bears, dusky langurs, gibbons, leopards (northern mountains); Asian elephants (northern preserves); geckos (northeast); water buffalo (Central Plain); macaques (southern islands); Burmese pythons, golden tree snakes, reticulated pythons (throughout Thailand)

CAPITAL CITY: Bangkok

OFFICIAL LANGUAGE: Thai

POPULATION: about 67,800,000

GLOSSARY

foothill: the lowest part of a mountain chain

goods: things to sell

isthmus: a narrow strip of land that connects two larger landmasses

maize: corn

map: a drawing or chart of all or part of Earth or the sky

monsoon: a strong wind that blows from the ocean toward land and brings heavy rains

mountain: a part of Earth's surface that rises high into the sky

peninsula: land almost completely surrounded by water

plain: flat or gently rolling land

plateau: a high, flat area

rain forest: a wooded area with a large amount of yearly rainfall

TO LEARN MORE

BOOKS

Morris, Ann. *Tsunami: Helping Each Other*. Minneapolis: Millbrook Press, 2006. This book tells the true story of a Thai family that survived the 2004 tsunami.

Taylor, Trace. *Asian Elephants*. King of Prussia, PA: ARC Press, 2008. This book talks about the elephants that live in Thailand.

WEBSITES

Enchanted Learning

http://www.enchantedlearning.com/asia/thailand/flag
This site has pages to label and color of Thailand and its flag.

Palaces of the King

http://www.palaces.thai.net
At this site, kids can go on a tour of several of the most important Thai royal palaces.

Thailand for Kids

http://www.kids-online.net/world/thailand.html
This site allows kids to hear Thailand's national anthem.

Time for Kids

http://www.timeforkids.com/TFK/teachers/aw/ns/main/0,28132,1156558,00.html
This general site has a section on Thailand that includes a quiz, pictures, and a timeline.

INDEX